Boutis & Trapunto

To my daughter

Catherine Coget

Boutis & Trapunto

SEARCH PRESS

INTRODUCTION
boutis & trapunto

I was introduced to embroidery and needlework when I was just six years old by my Aunt Eve. She was a talented needlewoman and she encouraged me to learn by showing me how to sew and work simple stitches. With her help I was soon able to produce my first piece of needlework and I have loved working with fabric and threads ever since.

While I was a student I still found time to explore many different techniques. I loved experimenting with colours, discovering new materials and working with different types of thread.

One day, while browsing in the library, I discovered an old illustrated book which contained one chapter about boutis. It contained wonderful photographs showing traditional hand-worked quilts beautifully embellished with a network of ornate symbolic designs. I was amazed by the detail and fascinated by the timeless quality of the work.

Enthralled and inspired, I read the chapter and decided to learn as much as I could about boutis. Over time I developed my own version, combining other methods of working — Trapunto and Marseilles Piqué, to produce beautiful pieces of quilting and embroidery.

It is worth while taking the time to learn these techniques. The results are stunning, stylish, creative and each design can be adapted to suit your requirements - whether you want something decorative for your home or something functional such as a cushion, quilt, tablecloth or bag.

This book is dedicated to all the many amongst you who will discover the same joy and inspiration that I have experienced over the years. These raised and padded designs, ornate and of great quality have given me an endless source of pleasure and I hope that you too will be inspired to create your own designs .

TECHNIQUES
boutis, piqué & trapunto

Provençal boutis, Marseilles piqué and trapunto are traditional techniques and they are used to create beautiful white, quilted and embroidered designs. These timeless techniques can be used individually, or together, to create attractive, highly ornate designs, or they can be used to decorate many different items for the home.

PROVENCAL BOUTIS

Provençal boutis – also called Marseilles embroidery, consists of the joining together of two pieces of the same white fabric, using tiny white stitches. These are used to outline motifs inspired by nature or everyday life and the motifs are then padded using quilting cotton. Pieces worked in this way are usually as beautifully stitched on the back as on the front, making them virtually double-sided. They also have a background pattern of corded channels, sometimes referred to as vermicelli work, usually worked on the diagonal and filled in with quilting cotton.

The finest examples of Provençal boutis are mainly worked on very delicate fabrics, usually cotton percale or batiste. When work is held up to the light, the padded motifs contrast beautifully with the transparent backgrounds and the elegant patterns are exquisitely highlighted with their delicate stitched outlines.

Before starting this technique you might want to look at some traditional boutis work. You may find some fine examples in a museum or you may be lucky and discover pieces in a second hand or antique shop. Hopefully they will be elaborate and highly detailed, with motifs and corded channels covering the whole surface of the fabric. The motifs used were highly symbolic, recounting episodes in the life of the embroiderer – hearts representing love, pineapples hospitality, and flowers beauty. These simple motifs were usually surrounded by vermicelli work – corners, curves, whorls and circles. Borders were usually completed with lines, scales or scallops.

MARSEILLES PIQUE

Marseilles piqué is as beautiful as boutis work, although finished items are heavier and they are not transparent. Three layers of fabric are used – the top usually cotton, a middle layer of wadding and a backing cotton fabric. A longer stitch is required for the quilting than is used in boutis and the motifs are usually geometrical: squares, diamonds, mosaics etc.

Traditionally, French workers used lovely Indian printed calicoes, or plain fabric, usually white, and they made clothing, soft furnishings and covers. Today the fabrics used are often soft, faded colours which are reminiscent of the old Indian printed calicoes.

TRAPUNTO

Trapunto originated in Italy. As in boutis, only two layers of fabric are used, the difference being that trapunto is not totally reversible. The under layer is either cut and then restitched after wadding, or else is a loosely woven fabric so the threads can be easily prised apart to insert the wadding. The other difference is that the background is not corded as in boutis, but is left plain.

The trapunto can be worked first and then a layer of wadding and a cotton backing added, before further stitchery is worked through all the layers as in Marseilles piqué. This will bring the trapunto area out in extra high relief.

In this book projects which do not need to be worked on both sides – such as cushions, tablecloths and mats, use the trapunto technique.

Marseilles piqué

Provençal boutis, Marseilles piqué and trapunto can be combined to create cushions, bags, tablecloths and more — and you can also make beautiful quilts like the one above. The embroidery and quilting techniques work beautifully together. You will build up your skills as you work through the projects in this book, enjoying, as I do, the wonderful effects of transparency, contrast, relief and colour.

MATERIALS
& equipment

The beautiful boutis and trapunto work done in years gone by was usually worked on cotton. The materials shown on the next four pages cover all the traditional fabrics and equipment you will need.

MATERIALS

FABRICS

Plain coloured fabrics can be used if you want to create original designs, but traditional Provençal boutis is usually worked on white fabric. Plain white cotton batiste, fine white linen or silk can be used, depending on what you are making. You should always choose a fine fabric as this will make your work easier and it will therefore be more enjoyable. Also, if you like the traditional, classic look, you will be happier with your finished item. The same fabric is used on the top and bottom, as boutis has neither a right nor a wrong side.

Trapunto is usually worked on a top layer of cotton. The backing is normally a butter muslin, or a cotton/linen fabric with a loose weave.

PREPARING THE FABRIC

Before you start, you need to know a few things about preparing the fabric.

It is advisable not to wash your chosen fabric before beginning any of the techniques. Finished pieces can be washed afterwards, although never in hot water. You must take into account any shrinkage that might occur when you are measuring the fabric for your project. Cottons nowadays are often treated to make them more stable during the washing process, but if you have any doubts, do a test first on a 10 x 10cm (4 x 4in) sample and adjust the pattern sizes accordingly.

As it is always best to cut and stitch fabrics along the straight grain, note that most cotton fabrics can be torn along the grain. If you are using linen, pull out a thread first. This will help you to find the grain of the fabric.

THREADS

Quilting thread This is cotton and coated with wax. It slides easily through the fabric, does not knot and finished pieces look very attractive if this is used.

Tacking thread This is cotton. Coloured thread can be used if you want your stitches to be more visible. Otherwise, use white.

Sewing thread This is also cotton. You will achieve a neater finish if the cotton you use is of top quality. This applies whether you are hand-stitching or machine-stitching – both methods are used to make the projects shown in this book.

PADDING

Quilting cotton, quilting wool, thick twist cotton or knitting cotton These can all be used for boutis. Background cording, stems and delicate lines can be filled in with any of these materials. They can also be used to pad smaller motifs.

Wadding Cotton wadding is sold by the metre/yard. It is advisable to cut it up into thin strips. Do not use cotton wool as this is not soft enough. Synthetic material, such as toy stuffing, is ideal – and it is easier to work with in the initial padding stages.

Wadding is used to pad out large areas such as leaves or flower petals.

EQUIPMENT

NEEDLES

A **Trapunto needle** This is approximately 15cm (6in) long. It is thick and with a sharp point, which is excellent for quick and easy 'cording'.

Tapestry needles (Nos 18 to 22) These have rounded ends and are suitable for filling in short stems, delicate lines and diagonals.

Quilting needles (Nos 9 to 12) are short, fine and ideal for stitching layers of fabric together. If you are a beginner, it is advisable to use a No 9 needle to start with. The higher the number, the finer and shorter the needle, and it is therefore more difficult to use.

EMBROIDERY HOOP

If you are a beginner it is advisable to use an embroidery hoop, as this will enable you to keep the fabrics at the right tension. These hoops are available in various sizes from needlecraft shops and hobby stores. For boutis and trapunto, a 15cm (6in) hoop can be used.

Larger scale quilted and padded items can be worked on a quilting frame, but this will take up more space. None of the projects in this book are worked on a quilting frame.

If you cannot manage to work with a hoop or frame, take care not to pull too hard on the thread when stitching, so as to avoid puckering. Also, it is important to ensure that the layers of fabric remain flat.

If you are using fine fabrics it is advisable to carefully wrap the frame with fabric or ribbon before you start (see page 12).

You should never leave a piece of work in the frame for too long, as this could permanently mark the fabric.

THIMBLES

You will need thimbles to protect your fingers while you are working!

Use one thimble to protect the finger positioned beneath the work. This will allow you to push the needle back when stitching.

Use a second thimble to protect the middle finger of your other hand. This will help you to return the needle and it will ensure you have penetrated both layers of fabric with the stitches.

OTHER USEFUL EQUIPMENT

A small rubber ring This is available from needlecraft stores and is used to grip the needle as it is pulled through the layers of fabric.

A wooden manicure stick (box wood if possible) This is used for padding motifs and patterns. Don't lose it, because it becomes smooth and slippery with use and hence more and more valuable! Sharpen the end with a nail file.

A toothpick (box wood if possible) or cocktail stick for padding smaller areas.

Embroidery scissors Make sure they have sharp tips.

Pins These are used to secure layers of fabric before starting to tack.

A pencil eraser and pencils I use HB, 2B, B – which is less soft, and H (or an embossing tool or dry point marker, e.g. an old biro).

Tracing paper or dressmakers' carbon paper Designs are transferred on to fabric using these. I would recommend using blue dressmakers' carbon paper.

Ruler I use a 30cm (12in) or 60cm (or 18in) ruler.

SUMMARY

MATERIALS
- White cotton or linen
- Butter muslin, loosely woven cotton or linen for trapunto
- Tacking thread
- Quilting thread
- Cotton quilting thread, thick twist cotton, knitting cotton or quilting wool
- Cotton or synthetic wadding

EQUIPMENT
- Trapunto needle
- Tapestry needles (Nos 18 to 22)
- Quilting needles (Nos 9 to 12)
- Embroidery hoop
- Wooden manicure stick
- Wooden toothpick or cocktail stick
- Rubber ring
- Two thimbles
- Pencils HB, 2B, B, H (or an embossing tool or dry point marker).
- Embroidery scissors
- Pins
- Ruler
- Tracing paper or dressmakers' carbon paper
- Eraser

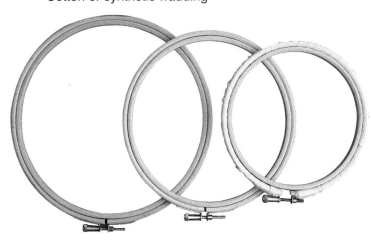

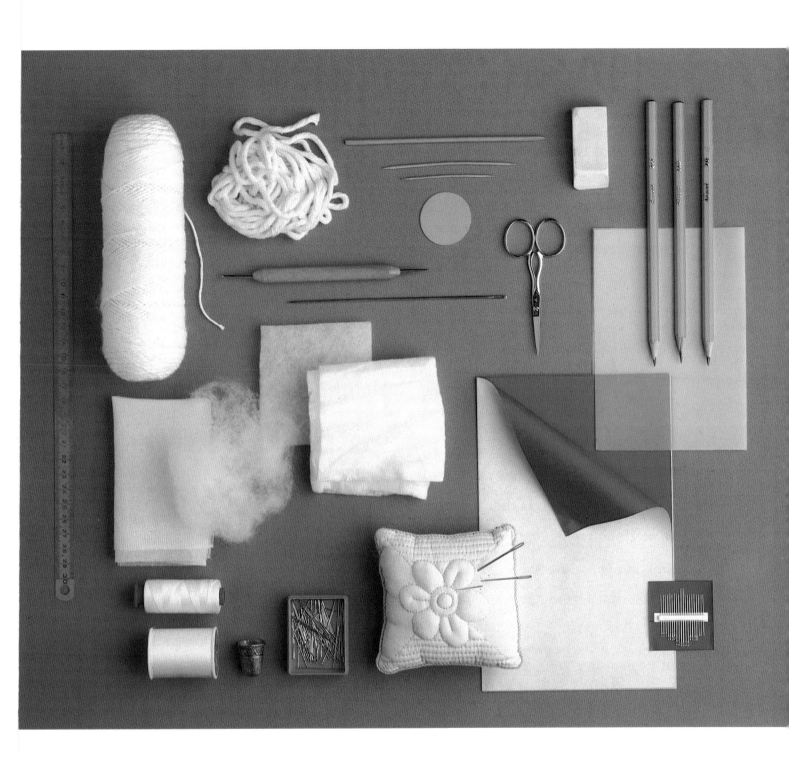

OUTLINING A MOTIF

When outlining a motif, no knots or stray threads should be visible. When you have finished tacking the two layers of fabric together, remove them from the hoop to start quilting (see step 4) then reframe them, positioning the motif in the centre. You will find it easier to stitch if you slightly loosen the tension with the hoop screw before you start.

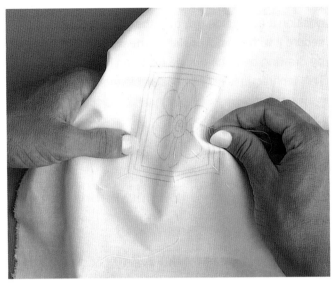

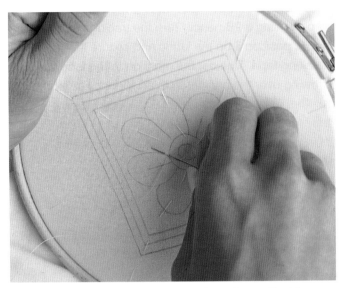

4. Thread a quilting needle with 50–60cm (20–24in) of quilting thread. Tie a small knot in the end, and slip the needle between the two pieces of fabric approximately 1cm (½in) from your starting point. Pull the needle up at the starting point and pull the thread through so the knot disappears between the two layers of fabric.

5. Now you are ready to start quilting. Start off with a backstitch.

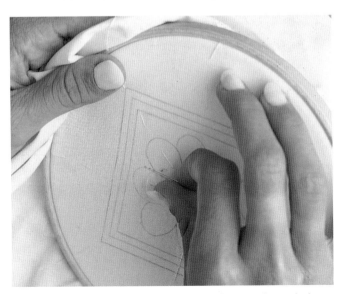

6. Outline each petal with small regular running stitches, completing each one before moving on to the next to ensure a continuous, even curve.

7. To finish a petal, make an invisible backstitch to complete the shape....

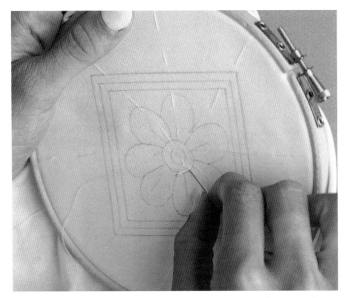

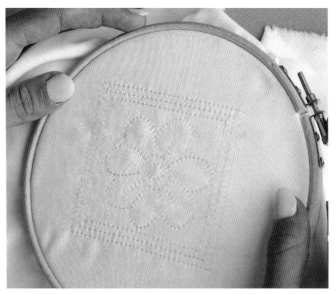

8. ...then tie a small knot in the thread very close to the fabric and push the needle back into the hole it emerged from. Pull the knot between the two layers of fabric. Trim the thread level with the surface.

9. The design must be completely stitched before it is padded. Continue working the centre with small regular running stitches completing the design as shown in steps 5-8, then remove the fabric from the hoop.

PADDING AND QUILTING

PADDING WITH WADDING

When padding, always work from the centre of the design towards the outer edges.

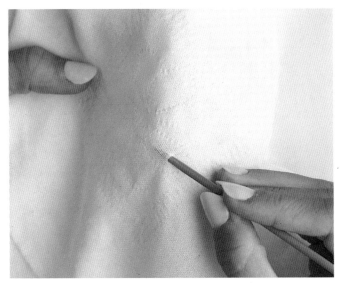

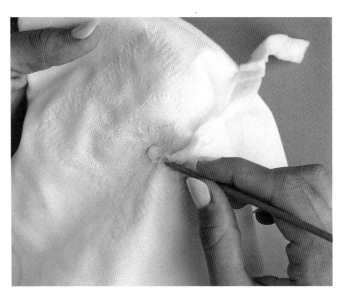

10. On the wrong side, use a manicure stick to create an opening beneath the centre of the design by gently parting the threads of the bottom layer of fabric.

11. Insert a small amount of wadding into the hole, pushing it gently through the fabric using small circular movements of the stick.

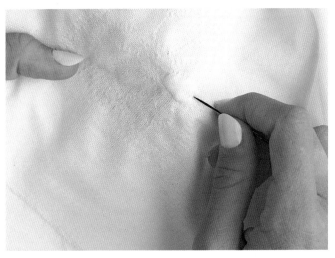

12. Push the wadding into the flower petal, filling out the tip and curves, but leaving enough space to be able to stitch up the opening. Using a tapestry needle, gently close up the hole, making sure the fabric threads do not get tangled up with the wadding.

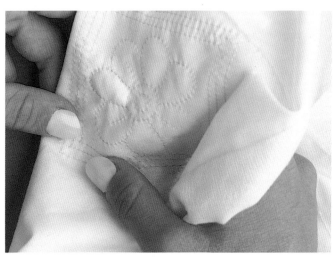

13. Even out the wadding using your fingers. It helps to hold the design up to the light; you can then make sure that all parts of the motif have been well padded. Complete the central design in the same way.

The density of the padding is a matter of personal choice. If the motif is too full of wadding, there is a risk of the fabric puckering, which would spoil the finished appearance. Padding should be plump, but not too hard.

PADDING WITH QUILTING COTTON

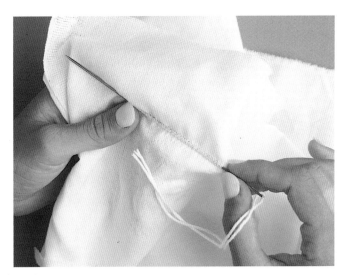

14. To pad a straight line, thread quilting cotton on to a trapunto needle; pull it through so it is double with even ends. Working on the bottom layer, feed the cotton in; repeat until padded. You may have to insert four to six strands, depending on the thickness of the cotton.

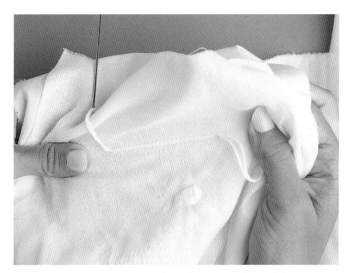

15. When you have completed one section of the border, stretch the two layers of fabric with both hands, to make sure that the quilting cotton completely fills the area.

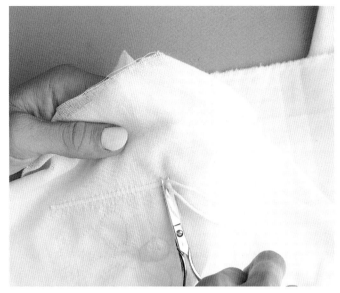

16. Carefully trim the quilting cotton level with the fabric at each end of the channel. Push any visible ends back into the fabric with the tip of a needle.

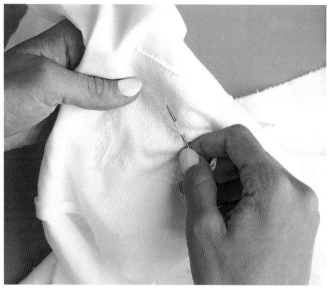

17. When padding a curved channel, thread quilting cotton on to a tapestry needle. Feed the needle into the area to be padded, up to the beginning of the curve, then bring it up to the surface of the fabric.

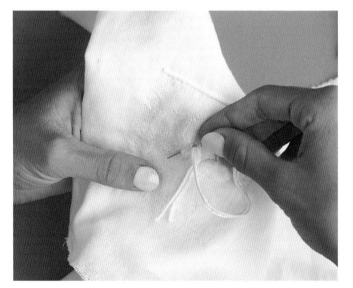

18. Re-enter the same hole with the needle and bring it up to the surface of the fabric further on. Repeat this until the channel is perfectly filled in. Trim the quilting cotton level with the surface of the fabric.

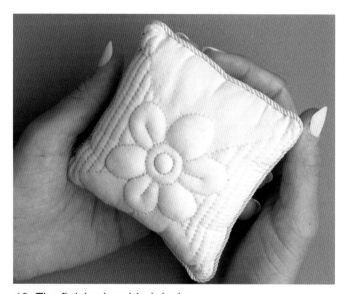

19. The finished padded design.

THINGS TO REMEMBER

The technique described on the previous pages is the boutis technique. The stitching and padding should always look perfect on both sides of the work.

• When working a boutis design, as the two layers of fabric are the same, you have to decide which will be the top and which will be the bottom. The padding is always done through the bottom layer

• With trapunto, only one side of the work needs to be neatly done. The other side is not usually visible, so you do not have to worry too much about knotted thread ends. After threading the needle the threads can be passed between the layers of fabric, alongside the design, avoiding any areas that are to be padded.

As with boutis, the padding is inserted through the back of the work.

When padding, to prevent an opening from getting too large, a small stitch can be made alongside the hole to strengthen the fabric.

• In this book, there is very little mention of cording (or vermicelli work). However, it is important to understand the method:

The cording for a boutis background is made up of straight lines drawn on the diagonal. These lines should be approximately 0.5cm (³/₁₆in) apart. If you are including it, incorporate it into your design either when you are initially transferring the motif (see page 15), or during the stitching of the design. The outline should be traced on a flat surface and must remain regular. You can vary the effect by adding broken or curved lines.

Always pad corded areas from the centre of the design, moving outwards.

This book shows you how to make thirteen projects, using boutis and trapunto. Clear, comprehensive instructions are given for each one, so they can be completed easily.

To help you improve your confidence and skills, I have calculated the level of difficulty of each project and have graded them as follows:

 **EASY**

 **MODERATE**

 **DIFFICULT**

Opposite: A beautifully worked traditional skirt

LAVENDER SACHET
trapunto

The photograph opposite shows the design above worked on two different fabrics: white linen and unbleached natural linen.

SIZE

Finished sachet: 21 x 21cm (8¼ x 8¼in) square.

EQUIPMENT

2B, HB and H pencils
No 9 quilting needle
No 18 tapestry needle or trapunto needle
Wooden manicure stick
Embroidery hoop
Sewing machine

MATERIALS

White linen: 24 x 49cm (9½ x 19¼in)
White butter muslin: 21 x 23cm (8¼ x 9in)
    for the backing
White butter muslin: 11 x 11cm (4¼ x 4¼in)
    for the small interior cushion
Small amount of wadding (cotton or synthetic)
Strand of white quilting cotton, thick twist cotton or
    quilting wool
White 100% cotton thread
White quilting thread
A4 sheet of thick tracing paper, 80gsm (55lb)
    or A4 sheet of dressmakers' carbon paper

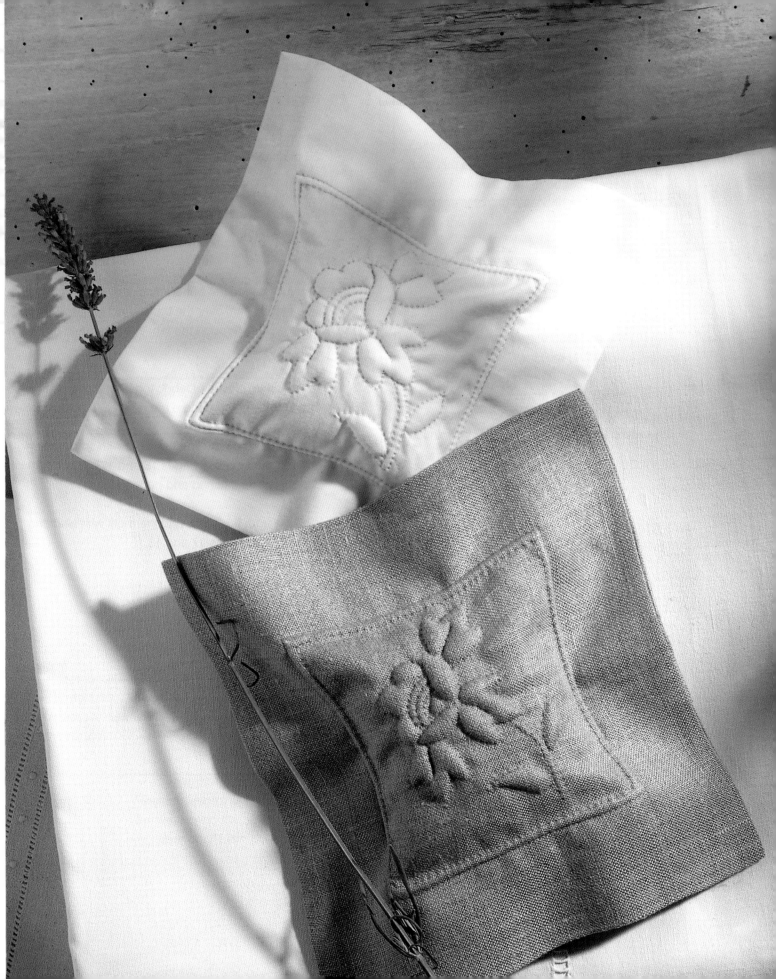

HYDRANGEA CUSHION
trapunto

SIZE
Finished cushion: 52 x 42cm (20½ x 16½in)

EQUIPMENT
2B, HB and H pencils
No 9 quilting needle
Trapunto needle
Wooden manicure stick
Embroidery hoop
Sewing machine

MATERIALS
Pad for a 40 x 30cm (16 x 12in) cushion
Unbleached natural linen: 98 x 55cm (38½ x 21¾in) –
    1.5cm (⅝in) seam included
Natural butter muslin: 42 x 55cm (16½ x 21¾in)
Natural quilting thread
White quilting cotton, thick twist cotton or
    quilting wool
Cotton or synthetic padding
Tacking thread
Natural 100% cotton thread
A4 sheet of thick tracing paper, 80gsm (55lb) or
    A4 sheet of dressmakers' carbon paper

The elegant borders of this floral design contrast
beautifully with the curved, padded shape of the
stylised hydrangea.

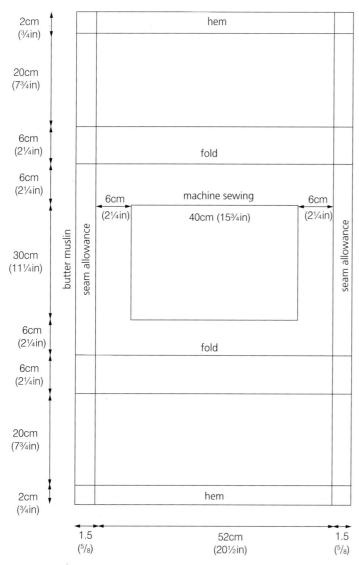

2cm
(¾in)

20cm
(7¾in)

6cm
(2¼in)

6cm
(2¼in)

30cm
(11¼in)

6cm
(2¼in)

6cm
(2¼in)

20cm
(7¾in)

2cm
(¾in)

hem

fold

6cm
(2¼in)

machine sewing

40cm (15¾in)

6cm
(2¼in)

butter muslin

seam allowance

seam allowance

fold

hem

1.5
(⅝)

52cm
(20½in)

1.5
(⅝)

Diagram 2.1
Pattern for the Hydrangea cushion

Note: Instead of tracing and drawing the motif on both sides of the tracing paper, you can use dressmakers' carbon paper (see page 15). This method is slightly easier, cleaner and quicker and the same results are achieved.

1 Using an HB pencil, trace the Hydrangea design on to tracing paper. Turn the paper over and trace around the outlines, on the reverse side, using a 2B pencil.

2 Fold the linen diagonally from corner to corner. Make a small centre crease where the folds cross.

3 Position the traced motif, reverse side down, on to the right side of the linen, and transfer it using an H pencil (see page 15). Refer to the diagram (left) to ensure that the motif is positioned correctly in the centre rectangle.

4 Carefully place the butter muslin rectangle on the reverse side of the linen, centering it over the pencilled motif, following the instructions in diagram 2.1. Make sure that the two layers of fabric are free of creases or folds.

5 Using tacking thread, tack the two pieces of material together.

6 Insert the fabric into an embroidery hoop (see page 15), making sure the two layers of fabric are not too taut. Using natural quilting thread, outline the hydrangea with running stitches; these should be as small and even as possible.

7 Working from the back and using a manicure stick, pad each flower and leaf with wadding. You may need to use a tapestry needle to fill in all the tips and curves (see pages 17 and 18).

Country Flowers Cushion - page 30

1. Following the diagram opposite, machine or hand sew the top and bottom hems, so each hem is 1cm (½in) wide.

2. Iron the fold lines, right sides together, as shown on the diagram opposite.

3. Fold the fabric right sides together, following the instructions in diagram 2.2 below. Make sure there is a 10cm (4in) overlap as shown.

4. Stitch along the seams AB and A'B' (see Diagram 2.2 below) 1.5cm (⅝in) from the edge.

5. Turn the cushion cover to the right side and iron the fabric carefully. Make sure that you avoid the padded areas.

6. Machine stitch a border 6cm (2¼in) from the outer edge of the fabric (see diagram 2.3), to create a decorative border. Insert the cushion pad

Note: The measurements given in the above steps include a seam allowance of 1.5cm (⅝in).

Diagram 2.3
The stitched border

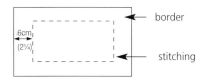

border

.6cm
(2¼)

stitching

If you would like a more decorative finish, two lines of cording can be added to the pillow around the outer border. This can be done after it has been assembled and sewn together.
Using a ruler, carefully mark two lines 0.5cm (¼in) apart around the edge of the pillow as shown in the photograph on page 27. Work small, even running stitches through both layers of fabric all around the border, then carefully pad each of the channels with cotton cord (see pages 18 and 19).

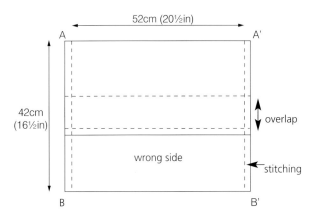

52cm (20½in)

A   A'

42cm
(16½in)

overlap

wrong side

stitching

B   B'

Diagram 2.2
Folding the cushion, showing the wrong side of the fabric with a 10cm (4in) overlap on the back .

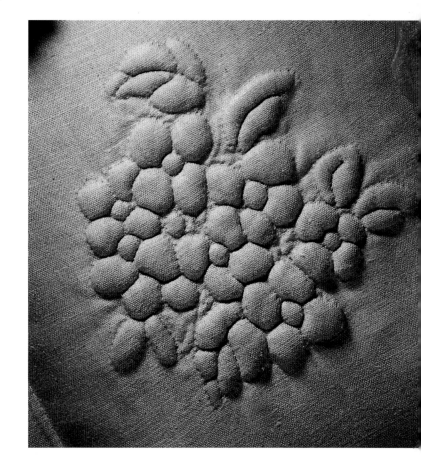

COUNTRY FLOWERS CUSHION
boutis & trapunto

Simple flowers are centred within a corded trellis design on this stylish cushion.

SIZE
Finished cushion: 54 x 54cm (21¼ x 21¼in) square

EQUIPMENT
2B, HB and H pencils
No 9 quilting needle
Trapunto needle and tapestry needle
Wooden manicure stick and embroidery hoop
Ruler and sewing machine

MATERIALS
White cotton/linen fabric: 57 x 125cm (22½ x 49¼in)
White butter muslin: 40 x 40cm (15¾ x 15¾in) square
White quilting thread and white 100% cotton thread
White tacking thread and white quilting wool
A4 sheet of thick tracing paper, 80gsm (55lb)
Cotton or synthetic padding
Pad for a 54 x 54cm (21¼ x 21¼in) square cushion.

Note: There is a little more to this project than the previous ones, but it is not difficult if you make the cushion in four easy stages:
1. Sew the top and bottom layers of fabric together.
2. Stitch the central flower and trellis design.
3. Assemble the cushion.
4. Mark out and stitch the border design.

ART DECO TABLECLOTH
trapunto

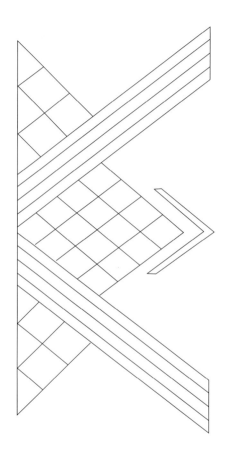

A decorative edge adds simple elegance to this beautiful white linen tablecloth.

CURTAIN TIE-BACK
trapunto

Daisies adorn this delightful tie-back which complements the plain curtain.

You will need double the materials listed opposite, if you wish to make a pair of tie-backs.

SIZE

Tie-backs are generally made in pairs. The tie-back in this project is a left loop. When made up and finished it measures 86 x 11cm (33¾ x 4¼in).

EQUIPMENT

Tracing paper
HB, 2B, H pencils
Quilting needles, Nos 9 to 12
Tapestry needles, Nos 18 to 22, or trapunto needles
Wooden manicure stick and cocktail stick
Embroidery hoop and embroidery scissors
Sewing machine with zipper foot attachment

MATERIALS

Natural coloured cotton: Two 90 x 15cm (35½ x 6in) rectangles for the tie backs
Natural coloured cotton: 70 x 36cm (27½ x 14¼in) for the ties and loop
Natural coloured butter muslin: 90 x 15cm (35½ x 6in) rectangle
Natural coloured cotton thread
Natural coloured quilting thread
Tacking thread
Synthetic wadding
Natural coloured cotton furnishing piping: 2.10m (7ft)

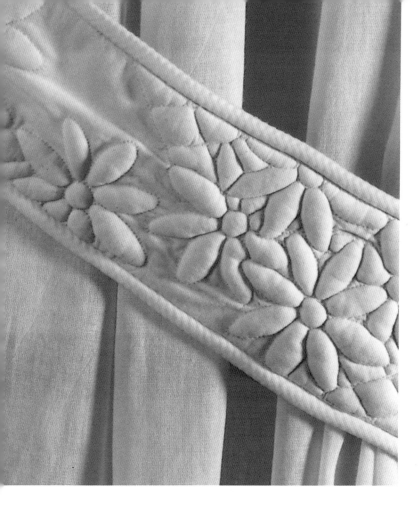

1 Using an HB pencil, trace the pattern on to tracing paper (see page 15). Turn the paper over and carefully trace around the outlines on the reverse side using a 2B pencil.

2 Fold one cotton tie-back to find the centre. Unfold it and position the tracing paper, reverse side down, on the right side of the fabric, placing the top right hand flower 1cm ($^3/_8$in) from the centre (see diagram 5.1 below). Reverse the pattern when making the right-hand tie-back and follow the instructions below.

3 Place the muslin on the reverse side of the fabric.

4 Carefully tack the cotton and muslin together, making sure they are free of creases and folds.

5 Frame the fabric and outline the design with small, even running stitches (see pages 16 and 17).

6 Working from the back, pad each flower with wadding (see pages 17–18).

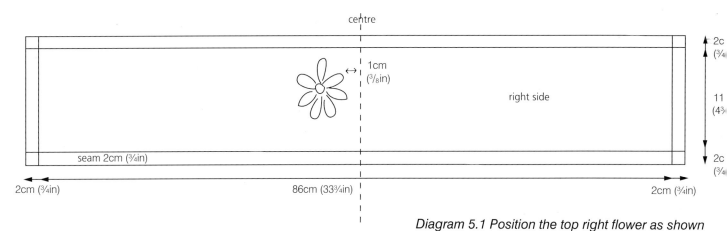

centre

1cm ($^3/_8$in)

right side

seam 2cm ($^3/_4$in)

2c ($^3/_4$

11 (4^3

2c ($^3/_4$

2cm ($^3/_4$in)

86cm (33$^3/_4$in)

2cm ($^3/_4$in)

Diagram 5.1 Position the top right flower as shown

Two ties and a loop are attached to the tie-back.

1 To make the ties, cut out two 70 x 12cm (27½ x 4¾in) strips of cotton fabric. These will include 1cm (½in) seams.

2 For the loop, cut out a 34 x 6cm (13½ x 2¼in) strip of cotton. This will include 1cm (½in) seams.

3 Cut out the tie-back lining: 90 x 15cm (35½ x 6in). This will include 2cm (¾in) seams.

4 The piping can be made by cutting the cotton fabric on the bias and wrapping it around cord (see page 75). Alternatively you can buy 2.10m (7ft) of natural coloured cotton furnishing piping.

5 Place the piping around the edge of the tie-back on the right side of the fabric, facing towards the centre. Tack and then machine sew using a zipper foot to get close to the piping.

6 Make the loop and two ties (see diagrams 5.2 and 5.3 below).

7 Fold the right sides together and machine each one with a 1cm (½in) seam. Leave one end of the tie-backs and both ends of the loop open. Turn through to the right side. Press with an iron.

8 Lay the ties and the loop on the trapunto surface of the tieback and pin them to secure. The raw ends will be caught in the piping seam when it is restitched (see diagram 5.4 below).

9 Cover with the lining, and stitch nearly all around.

10 Turn through; invisibly stitch the opening closed.

11 Press with an iron. Now make the right-hand tie-back following the steps carefully. Remember to reverse the design and the position of the tabs and loops.

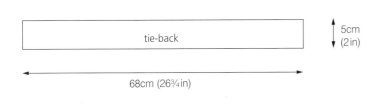

Diagram 5.2 Finished tie back folded and with stitched seams

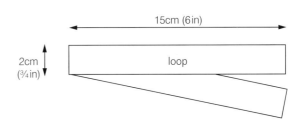

Diagram 5.3 The finished loop folded and with stitched seams

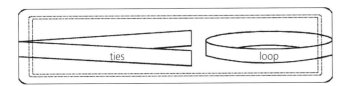

Diagram 5.4 Place the ties and loop over the piping on the trapunto side of the fabric

Diagram 5.5 The finished tie-back

PANSY BAG
trapunto

SIZE
This bag is 30 x 44.5cm (11¾in x 17½in)

EQUIPMENT
2B, HB and H pencils
No 9 quilting needle
No 18 tapestry needle or trapunto needle
Wooden manicure stick
Embroidery hoop
Sewing machine

MATERIALS
Natural (unbleached) and grey striped linen:
    41.5 x 63cm (16¼ x 24¾in) rectangle
Natural coloured linen: one strip 11 x 63cm (4¼ x 24¾in),
    and one rectangle 41.5 x 63cm (16¼ x 24¾in)
Natural coloured butter muslin: One strip 11 x 63cm
    (4¼ x 24¾in)
Tacking thread
Natural coloured quilting thread
Unbleached or natural 100% cotton
Quilting wool
Natural coloured linen cord for a drawstring:
    1.4m (4ft 7in)

These stylised pansies, curving around the centre of the bag, contrast beautifully with the natural striped fabric.

ZIGZAG BAG
boutis

The border of this small bag is delicately
highlighted with a padded boutis design.

This bag is 30 x 25.5cm (11¾ x 10in)

EQUIPMENT

HB, 2B, H pencils
Trapunto needle
No 18 tapestry needle
Quilting needle
Embroidery hoop
Wooden manicure stick
Sewing machine

MATERIALS

White piqué fabric: 28.5 x 63cm (11¼ x 24¾in)
 rectangle
White cotton fabric: 48.5 x 63cm (19 x 24¾in) rectangle
White quilting thread
Tacking thread
White 100% cotton thread
Quilting wool
Synthetic padding
Tracing paper
White cord: 1.40m (4ft 7in)

1 Cut out the white cotton lining – 48.5 x 63cm (19 x 24¾in). 1.5cm (⁵⁄₈in) seams are included.

2 Fold and press the fabric down lengthways, wrong sides together, 11.5cm (4½in) in from the top edge (see diagram 7.2). Unfold the fabric. The pattern will be transferred on to this border.

3 Using a 2B pencil, trace the pattern on to tracing paper. This is symmetrical, so it can be transferred directly on to the fabric (see page 15).

4 Transfer the pattern on to the fabric, 1.5cm (⁵⁄₈in) away from the fold, taking care that the zigzags line up at the seam.

5 Open the fabric fully. Place right sides together and stitch a 1.5cm (⁵⁄₈in) seam to form a cylinder.

6 Fold the fabric back along the original pressed line and tack together to secure the two layers.

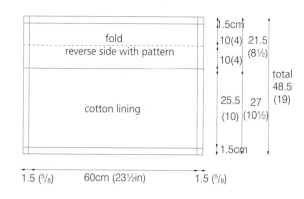

Diagram 7.2 Lining with boutis pattern on top edge

7 Outline the zigzag pattern with small, even running stitches.

8 Working from the reverse side, fill the channels with quilting cotton (see pages 18 and 19). The zigzags have sharp, right-angled corners, so fill each length separately, or you will end up with rounded points. Pad the other channels with quilting cotton or wadding (wadding is softer than quilting cotton).

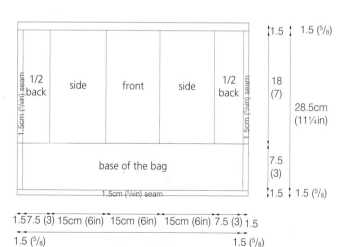

Diagram 7.1 The body of the bag

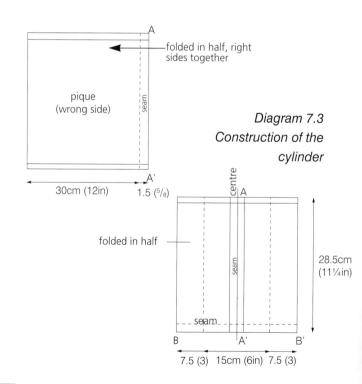

Diagram 7.3
Construction of the cylinder

Fold the cotton piqué, right sides together, and machine stitch seam AA' to form a cylinder (diagram 7.3).

1 Place the seam at the centre of the cylinder (see diagram 7.3) and press open.

2 Stitch the base seam BB' (see diagram 7.3).

3 Make a 15 x 15cm (6 x 6in) template for the base of the bag. Referring to diagram 7.4, position the template on the bottom of the bag to find the base seam. Trim the corners as shown and stitch the seams.

The interior cotton lining is stitched in the same way as the piqué exterior. Stitch the BB' seam, and then the C and D seams (see diagram 7.4). The padded pattern will be on the top edge of the cotton lining.

4 Place the piqué bag inside the cotton lining bag, right sides together.

5 Join the raw edges at the top of the bags with a 1.5cm ($^5/_8$ in) seam, but leave a 5cm (2in) gap to turn through.

6 Make two buttonholes for the cord 15cm (6in) either side of the back seam, between the two machined rows (see next step).

7 To make a channel for the drawstrings, machine stitch two rows, one 8cm (3¼ in) from the top of the bag and another 1.5cm ($^5/_8$ in) below this.

8 Slip two 70cm (27½in) cords through, between the rows; tie the two ends of each cord together and trim them both neatly.

9 Press the bag with an iron, avoiding the padded areas.

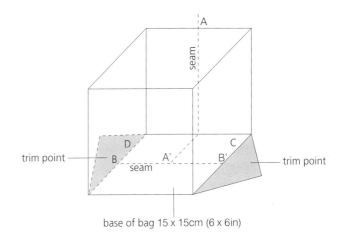

base of bag 15 x 15cm (6 x 6in)

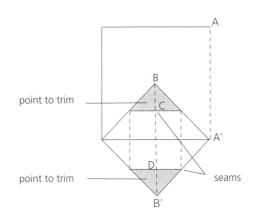

Diagrams 7.4 Piqué bag

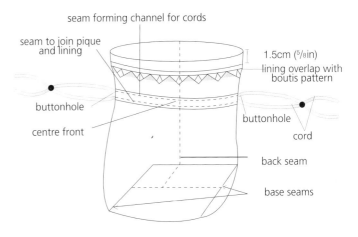

Diagram 7.5 The finished bag

SCALLOPED BAG
boutis

SIZE
Finished bag: 25 x 35cm (9¾ x 13¾in)

EQUIPMENT
HB, 2B , H pencils
No 9 quilting needle
No 18 tapestry needle
Trapunto needle
Wooden manicure stick
Embroidery hoop
Sewing machine

MATERIALS
White linen: 38 x 150cm (15 x 59in) rectangle
Cotton flannel: 35 x 50cm (13¾ x 19¾in) rectangle
White quilting cotton
Tacking thread
White 100% cotton thread
One white tassel
Synthetic wadding
Quilting wool
A3 tracing paper

A delicate padded border surrounds a stylised leaf design on this decorative envelope-style bag.

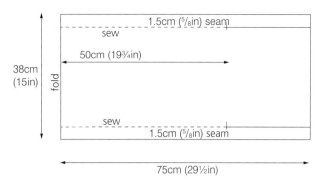

Diagram 8.1 Folding the rectangle

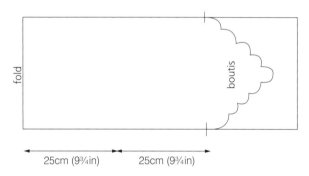

Diagram 8.2 Flannel slipped into the pocket

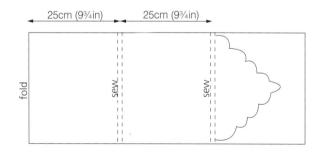

Diagram 8.3 The rows of stitches 25 cm (9¾in) apart

Before transferring the design and padding it, the bag has to be assembled.

1 Cut out 38 x 150cm (15 x 59in) of white linen. Fold it in two, rights sides together, to make a rectangle of 38 x 75cm (15 x 29½in). This includes two 1.5cm (⅝in) side seams (see diagram 8.1).

2 Machine stitch two 1.5cm (⅝in) seams along the top and bottom edges, but stop 50cm (19¾in) from the fold line as shown in diagram 8.1.

3 Turn it to the right side and press the seams.

4 Slip the flannel into the envelope you have just created (see diagram 8.2).

5 Tack it in place.

6 Machine stitch two seams 4mm (⅛in) apart, first 25cm (9in) from the fold, then stitch another two 25cm (9¾in) away from the first seam (see diagram 8.3). This defines the edge of the bag and will be filled with quilting cotton.

7 Fold the bag as shown in diagram 8.4 to make a finished shape of 25 x 35cm (9¾ x 13¾in).

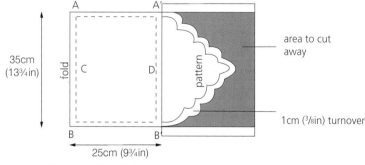

Diagram 8.4 Fold the fabric as shown

1 The design is worked on the remaining 25cm (9¾in) of the bag.

2 Referring to diagram 8.5, snip the corners of the design to open up the side seams.

3 Using a 2B pencil, trace the pattern on to tracing paper. This is symmetrical, so it can be transferred directly on to the fabric (see page 15).

4 Position the tracing paper, reverse side down, on the upper side of the bag and carefully transfer the pattern on to the surface of the fabric.

5 Tack the two layers of fabric together. This will keep them secure while you are working on the outline of the design.

6 Insert the fabric into an embroidery hoop to ensure an even tension. Carefully outline the pattern with small running stitches following all the contours (see pages 16 and 17).

7 Using a manicure stick, pad each area of the outlined work with wadding (see pages 17 and 18). When you have finished, hold the bag up to the light to check that all the points have been completely filled.

1 Referring to diagram 8.4, machine stitch the side seams AA' and BB' as shown.

2 After the pattern is outlined and padded, carefully trim the fabric 1cm (½in) away from the scalloped edge (see diagram 8.4). Notch the scallops and turn the edge of the fabric under to cover the raw edge.

3 Using an invisible slip stitch, complete the hem.

4 Referring to diagram 8.6 below, push quilting cotton through the edge of the scallop and the top and bottom of the bag at C and D.

5 Sew a tassel on to the tip of the flap. Press the bag, avoiding the padded areas.

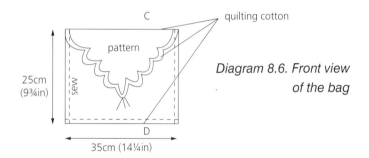

Diagram 8.6. Front view of the bag

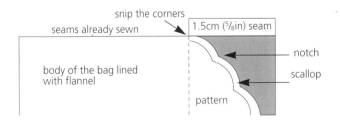

Diagram 8.5 Corner detail of the bag and of the motif

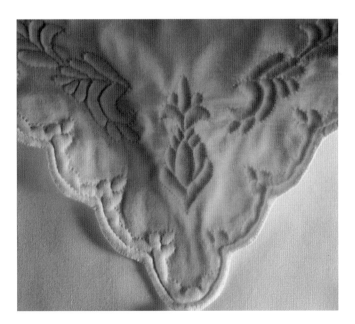

TORTOISE

trapunto

The shell pattern on this charming tortoise is worked on natural coloured linen.

EQUIPMENT

No 9 quilting needle
Tacking needle
Trapunto needle
No 18 tapestry needle
Embroidery hoop
Wooden manicure stick
Tracing paper
HB, 2B, H pencils
Sewing machine

MATERIALS

White linen: 50 x 50cm (19¾ x 19¾ in) rectangle
Natural coloured linen: 25 x 25cm (9¾ x 9¾ in) rectangle
Butter muslin: 25 x 25cm (9¾ x 9¾ in) rectangle
Natural coloured quilting thread
White 100% cotton thread
Quilting cotton
Synthetic wadding

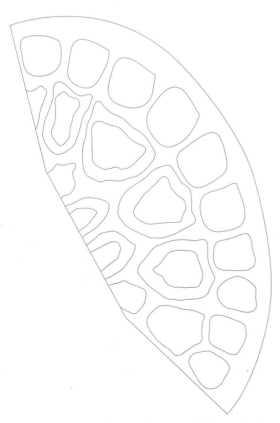

Diagram 9.2

BABY BEAR
trapunto

EQUIPMENT
No 9 quilting needle
Tacking needle
Trapunto needle
No 18 embroidery needle
Embroidery hoop
Wooden manicure stick
Tracing paper
HB, 2B, H pencils
Sewing machine

MATERIALS
White linen: 50 x 150cm (19¾ x 59in) rectangle
White butter muslin: 10 x 150cm (4 x 59in) rectangle
White 100% cotton thread
White quilting thread
Tacking thread
Quilting wool
Synthetic wadding
One skein of brown stranded embroidery cotton for the
   eyes and mouth

Baby bear's heart is there for everyone to see,
charmingly stitched on white linen.

CLEMENTINE PLACE MAT
trapunto

This stylised clementine design is the perfect complement to a natural linen place mat.

1. Using an HB pencil, trace the clementine design on to tracing paper. Turn the paper over and trace around the outlines using a 2B pencil.

2. Place the paper, reverse side down, on the top left side of the 25 x 35cm (9 x 13¾in) cotton fabric.

3. Using an H pencil, draw over the outlines, and transfer the design on to the surface of the fabric.

4. Place the butter muslin on the reverse side.

5. Carefully tack the two pieces of fabric together, making sure they are crease-free.

6. Insert the fabrics into an embroidery hoop and outline the design with small, even running stitches.

7. Work through the back of the muslin and pad the clementines with wadding. Pad the leaves and stems with quilting wool (see pages 17-19).

Diagram 11.1 The clementine design

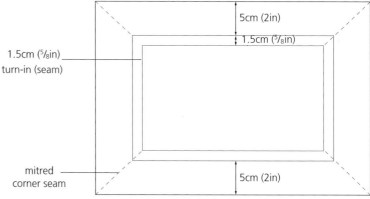

1.5cm (⅝in) turn-in (seam)

5cm (2in)

1.5cm (⅝in)

mitred corner seam

5cm (2in)

Diagram 11.2 Backing for the natural linen place mat

1 Following diagram 11.2 on page 76, mitre the corners of the linen 45 x 55cm (17¾ x 21¾in) – the place mat backing.

2 Using a steam iron, press under a 1.5cm (⅝in) to form a hem around the border (see diagram 11.2).

3 Carefully position the cotton fabric containing the padded orange and leaf design within the mitred border.

4 Tack the two pieces of fabric together.

5 Top-stitch 2mm (¹⁄₁₆in) in from the border edge (see diagram 11.3).

6 Press with an iron.

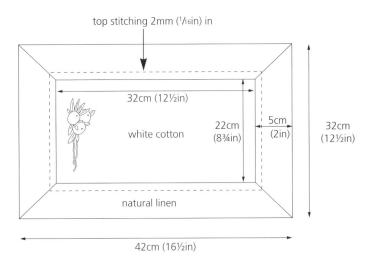

top stitching 2mm (¹⁄₁₆in) in

32cm (12½in)

white cotton

22cm (8¾in)

5cm (2in)

32cm (12½in)

natural linen

42cm (16½in)

Diagram 11.3
Final measurements

BIRDS WINDOW PANEL
boutis

The panel can be adjusted to the size of your window.

EQUIPMENT

2B, HB and H pencils
No 9 quilting needle
Trapunto and tapestry needles (fine)
Wooden manicure stick
Embroidery hoop
Sewing machine

MATERIALS

Fine white linen: 67 x 100cm (26¼ x 39¼ in) rectangle:
   adjust the size to fit your window
Tacking thread
White quilting thread
White 100% cotton thread
Quilting wool

*Full of movement and life, these graceful birds
fly across the bottom of this window panel.*

MEDALLION QUILT

trapunto

These graceful stylised flowers complement the beautiful blue floral design on this fresh and original quilt.

SIZE

Finished quilt: 118 x 118 cm (46½ x 46½ in)

EQUIPMENT

HB, 2B, H pencils
No 9 quilting needle
No 18 tapestry needle
Wooden manicure stick
Embroidery hoop
Sewing machine

MATERIALS

Printed fabric: 140 x 140cm (54 x 54in) square
    plus a 40 x 140cm (15¾ x 54in) rectangle
Natural coloured cotton : 55 x 55cm (21¾ x 21¾in)
    square plus a 55 x 140cm (21¾ x 54in) rectangle
Natural coloured butter muslin: 55 x 55cm
    (21¾ x 21¾in) square plus a 55 x 140cm
    (21¾ x 54in) rectangle
Flannel: 118 x 118cm (46½ x 46½in) square
Wadding
Quilting wool
Coloured cotton twill 3cm (1¼ in) wide: 2.10m (2⅜ yds)
Natural coloured cotton twill 1.5cm (⅝ in) wide:
    3m (3⅜ yds)
Natural coloured 100% cotton thread
Tacking thread
Natural quilting thread
Tracing paper

1. For the centre panel, carefully cut out a 55 x 55cm (21¾ x 21¾in) square from the natural coloured cotton fabric. As some of the pieces of the quilt are assembled on the bias, an extra 2.5cm (1in) has been allowed for the seams.

2. Decide on the size you want the floral wreath design. If you want it bigger, then enlarge it and carefully trace the design on to tracing paper using a 2B pencil.

3. Mark the centre of the square of cotton.

4. Position the traced design centrally on the right side of the cotton. Carefully transfer the large ring of flowers on to the centre of the cotton fabric using an H pencil.

5. Cut out 55 x 55cm (21¾ x 21¾in) of butter muslin and place it under the cotton.

6. Tack the two fabrics together carefully, making sure they are free of creases.

7. Using natural coloured quilting thread, outline the design with small, even running stitches.

8. Complete the outlining: working from the back, gently pad the flowers with wadding through the butter muslin. Using a manicure stick and a tapestry needle, push the wadding right into any points or awkward shape. Leave enough space to be able to stitch up any openings, making sure the fabric threads do not get tangled up with the wadding. Even out the wadding with your fingers.

The triangles

Cut out two squares with sides measuring 49cm (19¼in) then cut diagonally in half for four B triangles from the 55 x 140cm (21¾ x 55in) rectangle of natural cotton fabric, with the 2.5cm (1in) seams added (see diagram 13.2 below).

Transfer the corner design on to the triangles, and follow steps 2–8 on this page, using butter muslin backing.

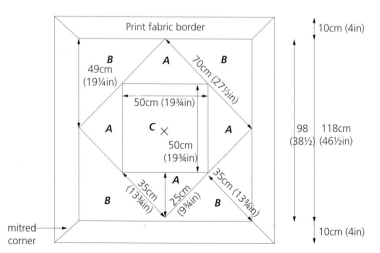

Diagram 13.1 Final quilt measurements

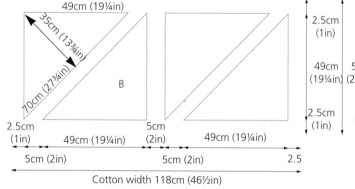

Diagram 13.2 Four B triangles including seam allowance

1 For the A triangles, use the print fabric. Start with two squares, 35cm (13³/₄in) on each side, and cut them diagonally in half to produce 4 half square triangles.

2 Referring to diagram 13.4, sew an A triangle to each side of square C with right sides together.

3 With right sides together, sew the four B triangles to the square formed by the A triangles, as shown in diagram 13.4.

4 Next place the blue cotton twill on the central square, along to the print fabric seam, and topstitch it 1mm (¹/₃₂in) from the edges. Carefully mitre the corners (see page 76) as you work around the inner border.

5 If you wish, further decoration can be added by stitching the natural coloured twill over the A–B seams where the triangles meet. Carefully mitre the corners as before and topstitch the twill down 1mm (¹/₃₂in) from the edges.

6 Cut out 118 x 118cm (46½ x 46½ in) of flannel.

7 Cut out the 140 x 140cm (55 x 55in) square of print fabric (this is the quilt backing) and, following diagram 13.4 below and the instructions on page 76, carefully mitre the corners so that the edges are turned over on to the top of the quilt with an 11cm (4¼ in) turning. This will include 1cm (³/₈ in) seam allowances.

8 Carefully tack the flannel to the back of the quilt top.

9 Position the flannel and top of the quilt inside the mitred backing, adjusting the layers of fabric until they fit.

10 Tack the fabrics together.

11 Top-stitch 2mm (¹/₁₆in) from the edge (see diagram 13.4). This will secure the flannel lining. Press with an iron, avoiding the padded areas.

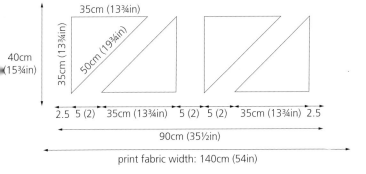

Diagram 13.3 Four A triangles plus seam allowance

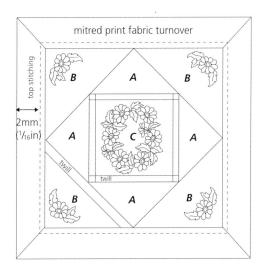

A: print fabric
B & C: natural fabric with
        padded design

Diagram 13.4 The quilt
pieces assembled

GLOSSARY
& seam techniques

WARP OF A FABRIC

The warp threads are the first to be stretched out on a loom, lengthwise. They are parallel.

WEFT OF A FABRIC

These are the strands which cross the warp threads, going backwards and forwards widthwise. The weft gives the width of a fabric.

BIAS

You find the full bias of a fabric by folding the warp thread over the weft thread. The bias is at 45° to the straight grain.

STRAIGHT GRAIN

The warp or edge of the fabric gives the straight grain of the fabric. There is no stretch in the straight grain of the fabric and the fabric does not become slack.

EDGE/SELVAGE

The edge of each side of a piece of fabric lengthwise.

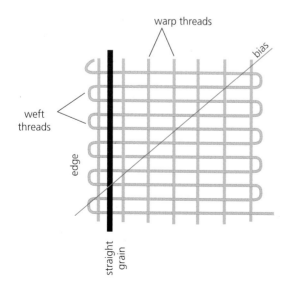

FRENCH SEAM

This is an enclosed seam. Place the fabrics wrong sides together. Make a first seam 0.3cm (¹⁄₈in) from the edge. Press the seam flat with an iron. Fold the fabrics back on one another, with the first seam serving as a hinge. Make a second seam on the wrong side, 0.5cm (¹⁄₄in) from the folded edge.

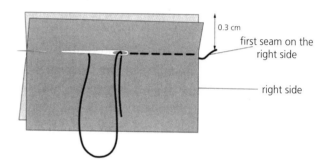

0.3 cm
first seam on the right side
right side

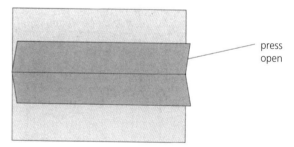

press open

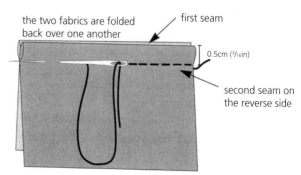

the two fabrics are folded back over one another
first seam
0.5cm (³⁄₁₆in)
second seam on the reverse side

RUN AND FELL SEAM

This is a strong flat enclosed seam. With right sides together, make a first seam 1cm (⅝in) from the edge (see diagram below). Trim one edge back to 0.5cm (¼in). Fold the fabrics back, with the first seam serving as a hinge. Fold the 1cm (⅝in) edge down and wrap it over the 0.5cm (¼in) edge to enclose it, then fold the enclosed seam down and tack in place. Machine stitch just inside the fold as shown. This is easier done from the wrong side, but it is neater if it is stitched from the right side.

DRY POINT MARKER

A tool which has two metal points. This can be used instead of pencils when transferring a design.

BIAS STRIP

Cut out strips of fabric on the bias with 1.5cm (⅝in) or 2cm (¾in) seam allowances, and add the amount of fabric necessary to enclose the cord you are using. Place the strips rights sides together, as shown in the diagram below, with a flat seam on the straight grain of the fabric.

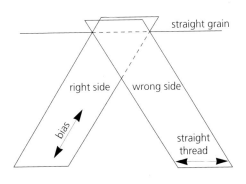

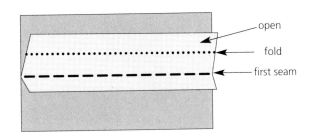

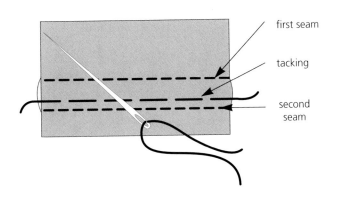

PIPING

Wrap bias-cut fabric around a piece of piping cord. Machine sew a seam close to the cord.

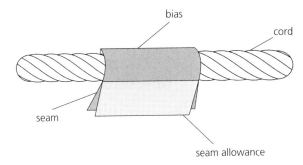

The motifs and beautifully worked patterns on this close up view of a traditional boutis piece are carefully worked on delicate transparent fabric.